PARASITES

TARA HAELLE

Rourke
Educational Media

rourkeeducationalmedia.com

Scan for Related Titles
and Teacher Resources

Before Reading:

Building Academic Vocabulary and Background Knowledge

Before reading a book, it is important to tap into what your child or students already know about the topic. This will help them develop their vocabulary, increase their reading comprehension, and make connections across the curriculum.

1. *Look at the cover of the book. What will this book be about?*
2. *What do you already know about the topic?*
3. *Let's study the Table of Contents. What will you learn about in the book's chapters?*
4. *What would you like to learn about this topic? Do you think you might learn about it from this book? Why or why not?*
5. *Use a reading journal to write about your knowledge of this topic. Record what you already know about the topic and what you hope to learn about the topic.*
6. *Read the book.*
7. *In your reading journal, record what you learned about the topic and your response to the book.*
8. *After reading the book complete the activities below.*

Content Area Vocabulary
Use glossary words in a sentence.

arachnid
host
larvae
malaria
offspring
parasite
parasitoids
reproduce
vectors
virus

After Reading:

Comprehension and Extension Activity

After reading the book, work on the following questions with your child or students in order to check their level of reading comprehension and content mastery.

1. *What are some symptoms caused by the Zika virus? (Summarize)*
2. *How many viruses does the Asian tiger mosquito carry? (Infer)*
3. *Why do insects drink the tears of other animals or humans? (Asking questions)*
4. *What do adult warble flies look like? (Text to self connection)*
5. *Where are some common places bed bugs are found? (Asking questions)*

Extension Activity

After reading the book, pick one insect and do some further research on its habitat, prey, predators, or any other interesting facts not found in the book. Record your findings on a piece of poster board. Draw a picture of your insect at the top. Color it in with markers and label all your information underneath. Share your findings with your classmates or friends.

TABLE OF CONTENTS

WHAT ARE PARASITES?

Deer Fly

Imagine having a tiny animal wrapped around your ankle or living in your stomach. Everywhere you go, it goes with you. Occasionally, it takes a bite out of you. That's what it's like to have a **parasite**. Parasites are creatures that feed off other animals without killing them.

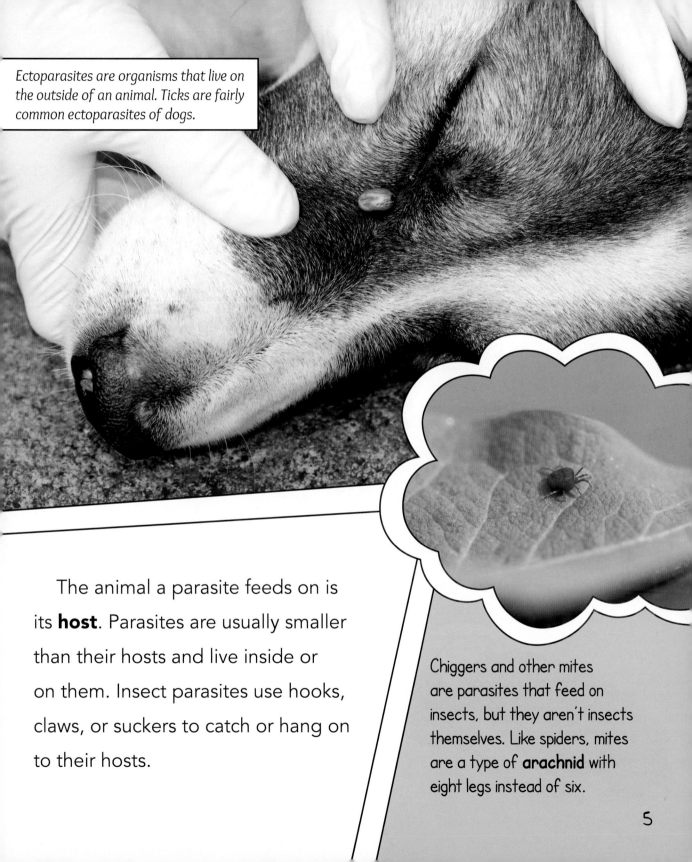

The animal a parasite feeds on is its **host**. Parasites are usually smaller than their hosts and live inside or on them. Insect parasites use hooks, claws, or suckers to catch or hang on to their hosts.

Chiggers and other mites are parasites that feed on insects, but they aren't insects themselves. Like spiders, mites are a type of **arachnid** with eight legs instead of six.

5

Tiny twisted-wing parasites have many hosts to choose from. They make themselves comfortable in silverfish, crickets, leafhoppers, ants, wasps, bees, cockroaches, mantises, or flies. For protection, they make a house of their host's body tissues. They can make their hosts infertile, or unable to **reproduce**.

A male twisted-winged parasite feeds on a bee.

The **larvae** of twisted wing parasites are some of the tiniest animals in the world, but there are a lot of them. Females may produce up to 7,000 **offspring**!

Alcon blue butterflies are brood parasites. Brood parasites are organisms that rely on others to raise their young. Alcon blue caterpillars start out eating plants and fall to the ground. Soon, red ants find them. The caterpillar's coating smells like baby ants, so the ants carry the caterpillar back to their nest. The ants adopt the caterpillars as their own and feed them. The ants' own larvae may starve at the same time.

Tachinid flies make up another group of parasites. The adults look like tiny houseflies. Immature tachinid flies are squiggly larvae called maggots. Their menu includes butterflies, moths, young beetles, sawflies, earwigs, grasshoppers, and other bugs.

Female tachinid flies have several clever ways to get their maggots into hosts. Some lay eggs near possible victims. The hosts swallow the maggots while eating leaves. The maggot then eats the host from the inside out. Other females glue or even inject them into their host's body.

THE BLOOD SUCKERS

You don't want the smooch of a kissing bug. These bloodsuckers feed on birds, reptiles, and mammals, including humans. But sometimes they transmit an awful illness called Chagas disease.

You have probably heard about vampires, monsters that suck blood. Vampires are not real, but many bloodthirsty bugs really do want to drink your blood!

In fact, just like vampires, bed bugs slurp people's blood at night as they sleep. These tiny bugs are pale brown when hungry. After filling up on blood for several minutes, they grow fat and purplish-red. Bed bugs can be hard to get rid of. They might live in homes, hotels, schools, stores, office buildings, and even libraries.

Lice are also common bloodsuckers. The feather louse prefers the blood of birds, but three other lice consume human blood. Head lice feed on scalps and cause itching. The body louse lays eggs on people's clothing. It hops to the skin when it wants a meal. Pubic lice live in areas with coarse hair, such as the pubic area or in facial, chest, or armpit hair.

Deer flies, stable flies, sand flies, and black flies also bite humans and other animals for blood. The wallop of a horse fly bite causes pain and a big welt.

Fleas are another blood-loving pest. More than 2,500 flea species exist. Some prefer birds, but most feed on mammals, including livestock and pets. Cat fleas find both cats and dogs tasty. They will even bite humans if they have a chance. Sand fleas live on tropical beaches and bite the soles of your feet or between your toes. They often remain just under your skin. The area swells painfully as they get bigger and grow eggs.

It's not blood that some moths, butterflies, and bees are after. It's tears! Some insects drink the tears of animals and even humans, probably to get more salt.

Not all these parasites prowl for human blood, though. Bat bugs look just like bed bugs, but they dine on bats instead. Warble flies, also called cattle grubs, feed on cows, horses, and deer.

Adult warble flies look like miniature bumblebees. They lay hundreds of eggs on a host's hair. When the larvae hatch, they crawl down and under the skin. Then they feed for months until breaking out of the skin as flies.

KILLER BABIES: PARASITOIDS

Tiny wasps lay eggs in whitefly larvae. The wasp larvae hatch from the eggs, and slowly weaken and kill the developing whiteflies.

Sometimes it's not adult insects that animals have to worry about. It's the babies who slowly devour their hosts over weeks or months. Many insect larvae are **parasitoids**. These young insects develop on or inside another animal just like parasites, but they eventually kill their hosts.

Tachinid fly larvae are one of the few types of fly parasitoids. Most parasitoids are wasp larvae. The boldest wasp parasitoids go after spiders much larger than themselves. Adult females inject venom into the spider to paralyze it. They drag it to their nest or lay an egg on or in it. The larvae suck, slurp, and munch away on the juicy spider.

Tarantula hawks are huge wasps that hunt tarantulas. The female stings a tarantula to paralyze it and drags it to her burrow. Her larvae then feed on the tarantula for weeks.

Another group of parasitoids includes ichneumon wasps, sometimes called scorpion wasps. More than 100,000 different species of ichneumon wasps exist. These wasp larvae gorge on beetles, flies, sawflies, spiders, scorpionflies, lacewings, and other insects.

The females lay eggs on a host's body, and the larvae penetrate the host after they hatch. Then they feast on their host from the inside out. Eventually they burst out of the host from all sides and kill it.

Braconid wasps prefer caterpillars, beetles, aphids, squash bugs, and stink bugs. Some of these wasp parasitoids might even control their host's behavior! *Cotesia* wasp larvae feed on woolly bear caterpillars. These caterpillars normally eat a variety of different plants. But when hungry larvae live inside them, woolly bear caterpillars fill up on the fattiest foods instead. The extra fat helps the wasp larvae grow even bigger.

The parasitoids cause behavior changes by affecting the hosts' decision-making and behavior control mechanisms.

Then there are the stunning but sneaky cuckoo wasps. Their bodies shine with gold and metallic green, red, blue, or purple. They are also sometimes called emerald wasps or jewel wasps. These sly beauties sneak into the nests of bees or other wasps and lay their eggs. The hatched larvae then steal the host's food or eat the host. They eventually kill the host's young, too.

MOSQUITOS AS DISEASE VECTORS

Have you ever come in from outside with itchy bites on your arms and legs? Your blood was probably a meal for mosquitos. These bites are usually just itchy and annoying. In many places, though, mosquitos carry fearsome diseases. Mosquitos that carry viruses are **vectors** for that **virus**.

In the United States, the *Culex* mosquito can infect people with West Nile virus. This infection feels like flu, and most people get better without long-term problems.

Ticks also bite humans and transmit diseases like Lyme disease and Rocky Mountain spotted fever. But ticks are not insects. These arachnids are closer relatives to spiders.

The mosquito species *Aedes aegypti* and *Aedes albopictus* carry many viruses that cause illness. These mosquitos prefer warm, humid environments and live mainly in tropical areas. Both have been found throughout the southeastern United States, too.

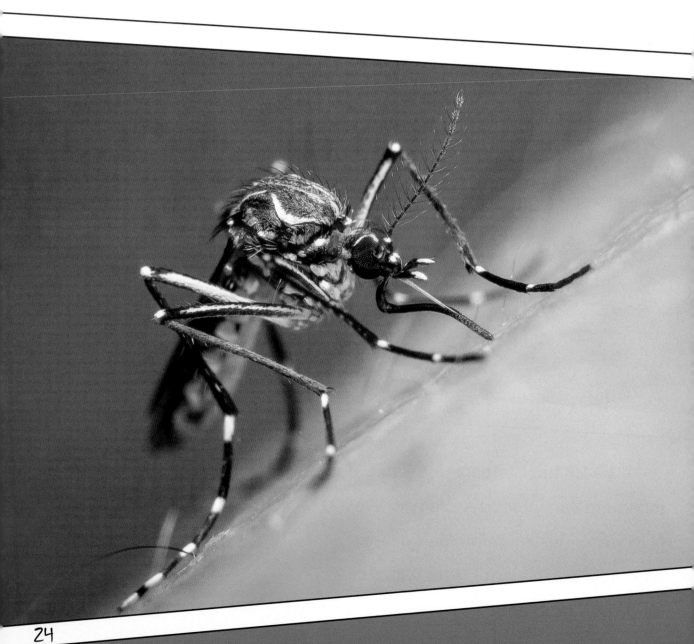

Aedes aegypti is called the yellow fever mosquito because it can carry that dangerous disease. The Yellow Fever Epidemic of 1793 killed more than 5,000 people in Philadelphia. Now, yellow fever circulates mostly in jungles and rainforests in Africa. A yellow fever vaccine can prevent people from getting this disease even if an infected mosquito bites them.

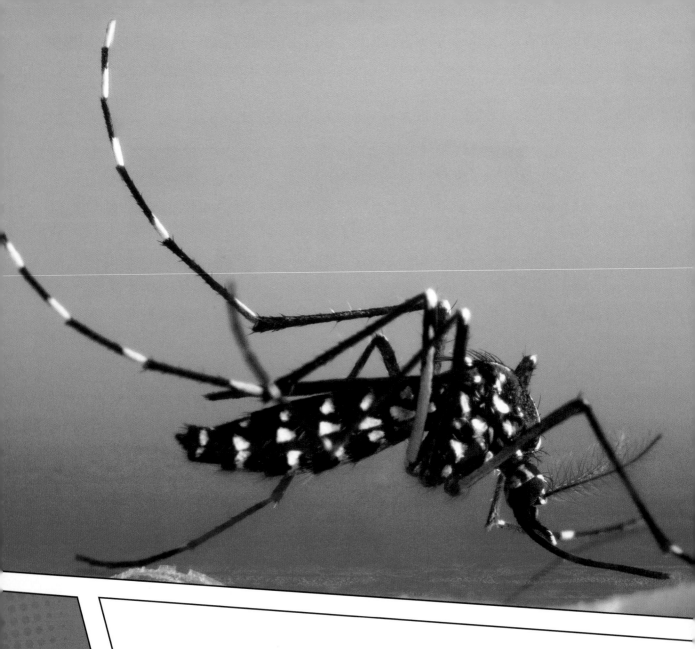

Aedes albopictus is known as the Asian tiger mosquito. It carries more than 30 viruses, but only some infect humans. Eastern equine, St. Louis, and LaCrosse encephalitis viruses are some rare diseases carried by these mosquitoes. Encephalitis is a swelling of the brain that can be deadly.

Asian tiger and yellow fever mosquitoes can also transmit chikungunya, Zika, and dengue fever. Dengue, called "break-bone fever," causes a high fever, rash, and muscle and joint pain. It's miserable, but most people completely recover.

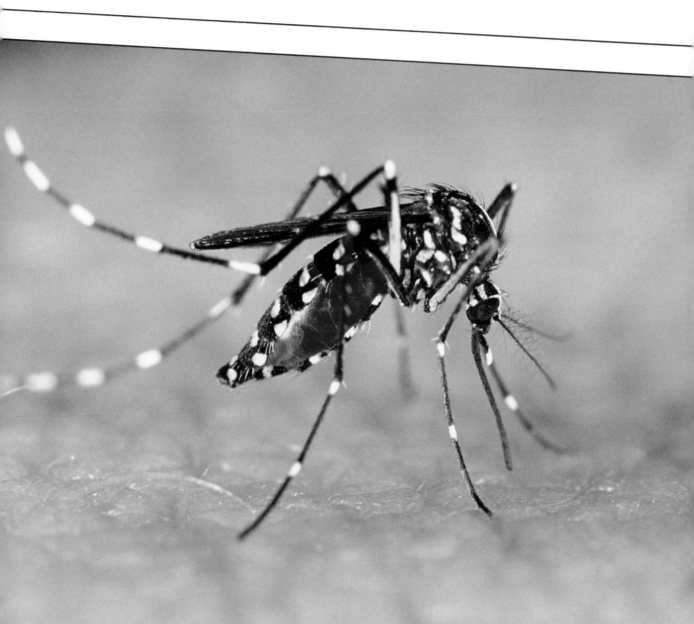

Fleas can also carry disease, such as the Bubonic plague. The oriental rat flea is one vector for plague. During some ancient epidemics, over 25 million people died from plague.

Chikungunya and Zika also cause fever, headaches, red eyes, a rash, and joint pain but are milder than dengue. Zika could be more dangerous for pregnant women because it might harm their growing baby.

The most destructive mosquito disease is **malaria**, carried by females of an *Anopheles* species. Almost half the world's population is at risk for malaria. Most people affected by it live in Africa, and scientists are working to help these people.

GLOSSARY

arachnid (uh-RACK-nid): an arthropod of the animal class *Arachnida*, such as a spider or scorpion; they have eight legs

host (hohst): an animal or plant from which a parasite gets nutrition

larvae (LAHR-vee): insects at the stage of development between an egg and a pupa, when they look like worms

malaria (muh-LAIR-ee-uh): a serious disease that people get from a particular kind of mosquito

offspring (AWF-spring): the young of an animal or a human being

parasite (PAR-uh-site): an animal or plant that lives on or inside of another animal or plant

parasitoids (PAR-uh-sit-oids): insects whose larvae live as parasites that eventually kill their hosts

reproduce (ree-pruh-DOOS): to produce offspring or individuals of the same kind

vectors (VEHK-turz): organisms, typically a biting insect or tick, that transmits a disease or parasite from one animal or plant to another

virus (VYE-ruhs): a very tiny organism that can reproduce and grow only when inside living cells; viruses are smaller than bacteria and can cause illness

INDEX

SHOW WHAT YOU KNOW

1. What is the difference between a parasite and a parasitoid?

2. Name some examples of parasites that feed on blood.

3. What kind of insect is the most common parasitoid?

4. What kinds of diseases can mosquitos transmit?

5. What are larvae?

WEBSITES TO VISIT

http://easyscienceforkids.com/tag/parasites

www.biocontrol.entomology.cornell.edu/kids.php

www.bedbugs.org/insects-for-kids

ABOUT THE AUTHOR

Tara Haelle spent much of her youth exploring creeks and forests outside and reading books inside. As an adult, she's traveled across the world on exciting adventures. She earned a photojournalism degree from the University of Texas at Austin so she could keep learning about the world by interviewing scientists and writing about their work. She lives in central Illinois with her husband and two sons. You can learn more about her at her website: www.tarahaelle.net.

© 2017 Rourke Educational Media

www.rourkeeducationalmedia.com

PHOTO CREDITS: Cover: © Marco Uliana, Steven Ellingson, Stephen Bonk; Page 1: © aaltair; Page 3: © Pavel Krasensky; Page 4: © Bruce MacQueen; Page 5: © thatreec, Jne Valokuvaus; Page 6: © Ian Redding, Melinda Fawver; Page 7: © Tartally A - Koschuha A - Varga Z, Elizabeth Spencer; Page 8: © Bruce MacQueen; Page 9: © Chinkc; Page 10: © smileus, nitat; Page 11: © Pavel Krasensky; Page 12: © Kampol Taepanich, Bruce MacQueen; Page 13: © Alice Mary Herden, Cosmin Marci; Page 14: © Visanuwith Thongon, Whitney Cranshaw - Colorado State University - Bugwood.org, zahorec; Page 15: © Pavel Mikushin; Page 16: © AJ Cespedes; Page 17: © Ian Redding, Vilainecrevette; Page 18: © InsectWorld; Page 19: © Stephen Bonk; Page 20: © Katarina Christenson, Eldie Aaron Justim; Page 21: © Aris Suwanmalee; Page 22: © Somyot Pattana; Page 23: © Mario Saccomano, Erik Karits; Page 24: © Torres Garcia; Page 25: © Jarvin Ontakrai; Page 26: © InsectWorld; Page 27: © Tacio Philip Sansonouski; Page 28: © Parinyabinsuk, Sergejus Byckovskis; Page 29: © Amir Ridhwan

Edited by: Keli Sipperley
Cover and Interior design by: Tara Raymo www.creativelytara.com

Library of Congress PCN Data

Insects as Parasites / Tara Haelle
(Insects As …)
ISBN (hard cover)(alk. paper) 978-1-68191-696-5
ISBN (soft cover) 978-1-68191-797-9
ISBN (e-Book) 978-1-68191-895-2
Library of Congress Control Number: 2016932572

Printed in the United States of America, North Mankato, Minnesota

Also Available as: